THE FABULOUS OP

The Fabulous Op

GARY BARWIN AND **GREGORY BETTS**

Text copyright © 2024 Gary Barwin and Gregory Betts.
Typesetting and book design copyright © 2024
Downingfield Press Proprietary Limited.
All rights reserved.

Without limiting the rights under copyright reserved above, in accordance with the
Copyright Act 1968 (Commonwealth of Australia) no part of this publication may
be reproduced, stored in or introduced into a retrieval system, or transmitted, in any
form or by any means (electronic, mechanical, xerographic, recording, or otherwise),
without the prior written permission of the copyright owner and the publisher of
this book, except for brief passages quoted for the purpose of criticism or review.

Gary Barwin and Gregory Betts asserts their right to be
known as the author of this work.

Book and cover design by M. G. Mader.
Cover illustration by Gary Barwin.

ISBN 978-1-7635569-4-2 (paperback)

First published April 2022.
Acquired and published December 2024 by

Downingfield Press Canada

an imprint of

Downingfield Press Proprietary Limited
Suite 346 / 585 Little Collins Street
Melbourne Victoria 3000 · Australia

For a full list of addresses and contact information, visit
global.downingfield.com

Downingfield Press undertakes its work on the traditional lands of the Wurundjeri
people of the Kulin Nation and pays respect to Elders past, present, and emerging.

A catalogue record for this work is available from the National Library of Australia

GARY BARWIN is a writer, composer, and multidisciplinary artist and the author of 26 books including *Nothing the Same, Everything Haunted: The Ballad of Motl the Cowboy* which won the Canadian Jewish Literary Award and *Bird Arsonist* (with Tom Prime) His national bestselling novel *Yiddish for Pirates* won the Leacock Medal for Humour and the Canadian Jewish Literary Award, was a finalist for the Governor General's Award for Fiction and the Scotiabank Giller Prize, and was long listed for Canada Reads.

GREGORY BETTS is a poet and professor at Brock University. His work consistently explores concrete, constrained, or collaborative poetics. He is the author of 11 books of poetry, including recent titles such as *Foundry* (Ireland 2021), *The Fabulous Op* (Ireland 2021, with Gary Barwin), and *Sweet Forme* (Australia 2020). His poems have been stencilled into the sidewalks of St. Catharines, Ontario and selected by the SETI Institute to be implanted into the surface of the moon. He performed at the Vancouver 2010 Olympics, as part of the Cultural Olympiad, and has travelled and performed extensively across Canada, the US, and Europe. He is the curator of the bpNichol.ca Digital Archive, and author of the award-winning scholarly monographs *Finding Nothing: the VanGardes 1959-1975* and *Avant-Garde Canadian Literature*.

v

OP
EM

PO

ME
PO

ME

EM
OP

I

(o)

p(o)etri

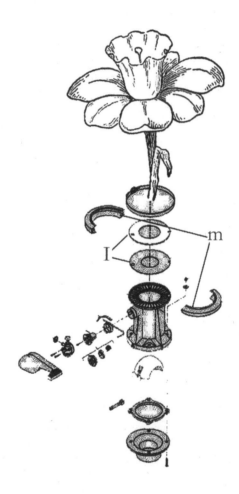

O this is a poem
about the dark mind
polylocalized
ragments
put your ear to the shall
we broke(n)

O this is a
poem become
minded whole
a great white
washed shall
adios
various radios
radiate variants
pliant plaints
record prophets
this wobbly planet
where poems
splint winds

O
O
paints
truth north
where all roads
lead to their
own wend
digs cruelty
throughts
olipsis
sussoration

I am
rose ellipse this
wendering nothing
in-sparkling nothing
onsettling in air
moorning

so sorry
garbage mine
a line subsplashed
faces in a lign

so sorry
expoundmaker
frogs fleen gravity
mo(u)rning

hunging (o)
un a line

a poem
can only
apologize
~~to politics~~

I contradicts my multitude
every atom tongue of it
flowers

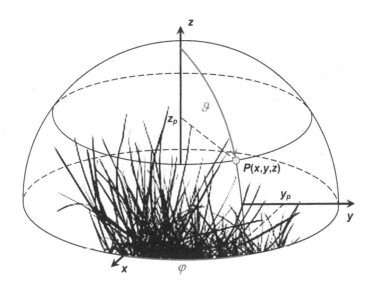

my
best regeneration
wants

you o me
apoemology

so(ng) its an
evermorover
(amoreverarmour)
reverer

or
drone angels
hum angels
smeared dreams

soon(g)
dust of(f) dust
the (f)ear of the
something

you me
less blue
hook me
graphed
racture
strophe
(en)crypted
'

ell inging
o I opened

blue
moa(r)ning
this pull
into

bookish dark
night cowered
gate of dirk
comma, then

placed
esllipsed
overydayzed

O this poem
when I found it
wendered naked

these letters ©lothe
sigh lens ools
the chance
magi of othing

will you run after me
embrace me, your and
the paraphrase

I rive
broken sense
bless this
little everything
partfection held in
(g)low

we do
something
something
and for which
    for watch
we o

re new
re new grief
re language rising
re broken laugh
re always

recomposing
as what you
riot
you art

time remained sign
inging like grief
all language
blood

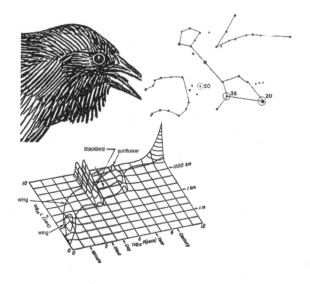

o pens we arrowed
do not imagi

mine the centaur
a jar is
where roads
ancient yellow
we are
two roads submerged
cient heaven
submagi

beh(old

ouds scud
reath of larks
shrapnel-could

we have ived long
awn ourns us
ilight gapes

brace
those we green with
et the ight ail

listen: else arkness rasp you
as clods rush our leep

our
poppy mo(u)ths
words o
s)wallow the entire night

the funeral baked
meats did coldly furnish forth
the marriage tables
—Hamlet

how the fur burned
Perseid-flamed
police officer

how distant [capitalism]
fled sonwards
ask tablets like
readed reat

[inaudible]
eaches [petals] we
were raid knowing to isk

in daffodil
poppying climate
changes

there you are
poem among twenty
snowy trees the moving ision

there you are
the cruelest math
maxing out desire

tree the rippled moth
melting light into desire

tree your are
a poem

scar or tree crinolines
moving the matchstick of desire

star or tree editating
the omission you desire

your celerity the memory
the cruelest math

the crumpled myth
the author a cruel mo(u)th

I park upon a tree

dark and requesting all sinced letters be turned
and all afternoon

snow)night

darkness I blackbird lost

recently opened lilacs
wending, ready
ready ready to
everything unsilenced

how

    only as cloud
               o poem has e®asured

beauty like

your sleeping head, listing
    my love

turning
        & turning
               the wedding

    true minds
    sea-lovely
looms and

               dreams outside

28

these sentences
eech fails speech
(feel. feel better.)

a sad a sad
      nothing was

woods these
      in the valley of

             utterly

surly bonds

      earth
overflows

I am sad o say I
      am sad
to say
    o

valley

                    y(our house

because I

                 for death go

                 go heart broken

strange things go midnight
                 blooms

your bedded tree

                 go

I lost

if

                        only this

go

            take
                light
                 ghost worded

see itself

                    you

seize itself

                    is

the atom the fish

                    a meadow

shrub

out amidst shadowy stars
               stairs

geomorphic rivers
            andscapes

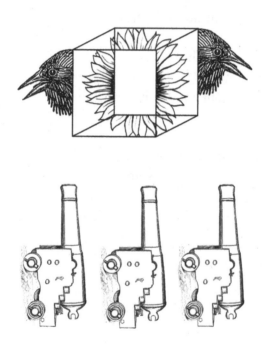

                          the bare

greye
            itss lowt highs

                    s nowy mounta ins
    or just after
              it gets pass edd
                          own
      rounds us

                      [weeping]
                      with its s(love)nly

rouse

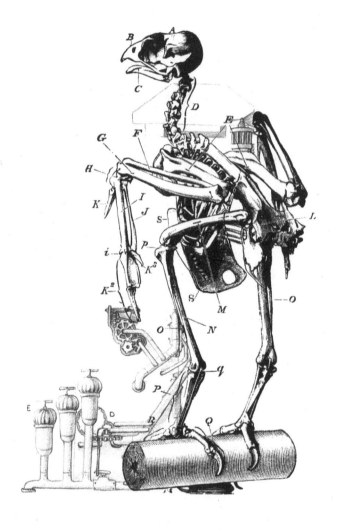

34

verything that signifies
grow old
let us hollow
        in our candid operations
let us
wing

                              hewn eye

loud they
night they
        do not scream

                              do not scroll

        hopping mishap piness

let us   humble torches
chapter yellow snakes of mourning
            less everything that signifies growl

36

II

word word word
word wodr wod r

wo rd wo dr wro d
wrod wrd o wrdo

wr do wr od wdor
wdo r wdro wdr o

wd or wd ro w odr
w ord w rdo w rod

w dro w dor ow rd
ow dr owr d owrd

owd r owdr or dw
or wd orwd orw d

ordw ord w od wr
od rw odw r odwr

odr w odrw o drw
o dwr o wrd o wdr

o rwd o rdw rwd o
rwdo rw do rw od

rwod█ rwo█d rodw█
rodsw roswd rosdw

row█d rowd█ rdo█w
rdow█ rd█ow rd█wo

rdwo█ rdw█o r█owd
r█odw r█dwo r█dow

r█wdo r█wod dwor█
dwo█r dwro█ dwr█o

dw█or dw█ro dow█r
dowr█ dor█w dorw█

do█rw do█wr drwo█
drw█o drow█ dro█w

dr█wo dr█ow d█wro
d█wor d█orw d█owr

d█row d█rwo █wdor
█wdro █wodr █word

█wrdo █wrod █odrw
█odwr █owrd █owdr

orwd ordw rdwo
rdow rwdo rwod

rodw rowd drow
drwo dwor dwro

drow drow drow

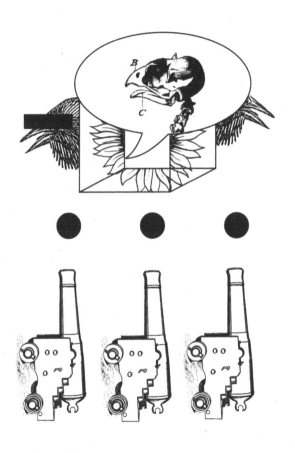

this poem
called itself

sunk a
twilight's glare

this poem left
we gleaming

oh you
spectral treaty

we see youre glory

griefly

you
little red rock
blue sea
under blue sky

O sons of weapons
we borrow

                              slit throats
                              poppy moats

bloody glowing
fierce laws

glean home lest

stars you sweep

> watched wave
> send
> queen against

we have lost
how people
lived

nothing is ███ everything is permitted
permitted is ███ nothing is everything

nothing is permitted everything is ███
permitted is ███ everything is nothing

nothing is ███ permitted is everything
permitted is everything ███ is nothing

not
the ink invisible

 rased or moved for
further study

but the page
the explorer

the poet
an exporter

a permanent tourist
a last stenographer

in fields of snow

                        like bonds

telling

my nosebag

no-one, midwif, tack, songbird

                              my nostrum, night to land on,
                                    rat jelly and wheel

weird worm and

                              unexpormidable caribou,
                                    my talc, sorceress

unthrifty loveliness
elegy, short haul, ecclesiastic and wheelbarrow
                              my worrying weirdo, sundial
                                                  bloom

these hours gentle
calm honey, my midpoint, talk

                                          my hunch,
                                spade, ecologist and
                                        wheelwright

let no ragged hand
wound welt someday disregard

                              my window and stone
                              militia, tick, soufflé

III

w are
living
 in
loose
in

whispering
whispering for show

how we the poem
open goodbye
sleep dictionaries

the I to apologize
north and tomb
blacklamb birdflies

this [grief] loosened
crooked sty
greenforces
a thrillsong [weep] in this poem

truce poem a grief heavy wood isthmus [break]

so much

    (so much) that
        good gentle night
            so much

gentlemoon good
    pleasure [grief]

                good

[such grief]
    so much

[grief] pleasure

so much

nevermore[

                    ]nevermore

 evermore(

)remover

no more veneer{

                    ]no more nerve

omen(

                    ]norm

more(

)even

no nor{

            ]ever

its precient deathware

toll

a head undressed

no sorrow pardons

wounding sound

shelter none shorenosed ache

anchor's bind to shore

stoop
grown in air

borrowed warnings

groan

parsing

death
moon

angry

machine towards
time's narrow

frown box
blue

fragments

raith

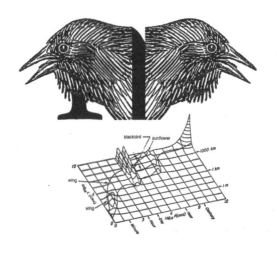

the moon undressed
        thirsty dread

           anchor's ache

rains
     snares

lands and talk
       the user

          sand white

    quatrain

            arrows ware

a poem is only
to love songs

death
an ethic
fire heat water
    ice

in sorrow

forge

time shattered
into crowns and homilies

mark war

another scrawl

be kind to old shalls
that poetry abandoned

shudder clown

lost

quaint old sun

I have

angry kindness

ah, no no
we shell write again

Oxymandius I thought
        the king had more control

and how you are photos of recent
        scenes of silence

are you a good person
        I need help
imagine lover's legs
        alone in rackless lace

face half sunk
        sand
        weeping jaw

needling forehead
        broke llipses
        speaking name

passions easy as magazine
        in a doctor's office
        help

her with help
        money

        just as the next spam appears

my name is Nata$ha

have pics to share
ask for poetry

    look at me
          boundless and are
          or
[grief]

          you never goes away

these poems together
you ask me
what would leaf and shoe write
    what would worldly paradise look like?
I fall on
shampoo bottles dew-brindled, lost
        earth-visible stars
parking spot, paring knife
        a crock of cash receipts, shadows
woe and wealth
        disposable razors in the river
earnestness and game

you ask me what
leaf and shoe like

sweet like glue
              ripped tiles of such root
leaf and spine
              lightning's flute

all you need is

there's nothing you can say
that can't be need-

ed

IV

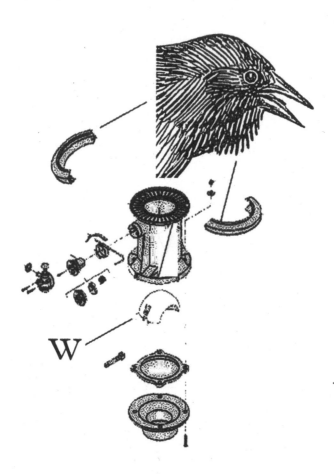

W

repeat
after me
this

is a totally ███
poem
a totally ███

not read
███ not read ███

it says it █peaks
███ like
███ the stars like

don't █ the poem fool you
don't ███ poem fool

you try ███
again try to ███ again

this ███ is repeat after me:

water a short sad brook
leaf ███ its shadow

███ out of someone's ███
a page
I can't remember ███
I can't ███

organize

that organize
[weeping-   -weeping]

I try to co
ntain it I try to
but

now

but   repeat

on a fallen apostrophe
        gathered
      the world

are you happy to
the poem never more
    itself

its horrible
legacies of service

destroy it

        warshippers

fracture

           let them roar

lake water

          lapping low
          destroy

let them roar

        always fragments in these
        ellips of linnet's wings

a-glimmer

        purpling glow

let them row now
veils

        crickets fragment

let figments

        cracks in turtle shell

let them

this poem inten-
tionally left
▮*

*▮

I have eaten

            angel nature

mourning

      the machinery of
           hollow eyes

forgive me

   broken earth

   rekins

   and you
   mouth
   to me
   that the
   poems
   can begin
   again)st

I have eaten

           angel nature

mourning

      the machinery of
           hollow eyes

forgive me

   broken earth

   rekins

   and you
   mouth
   to me
   that the
   poems
   can begin
   again)st

Milton Keynes UK
Ingram Content Group UK Ltd.
UKHW022323011224
451695UK00007B/51